On Thinking About It

Also by John R. Sabine and published by Ginninderra Press
Around the World in Eighty Ways
Slam Dunk Poetry (Pocket Poets)

John R. Sabine

On Thinking About It

Acknowledgements

Some of these poems have been previously published as follows: 'On explaining poetry (to the very young)', 2010, *Common Ground* (Poetry in the community No. 2), Ginninderra Press; 'Time Heals All', *Selected Works of Our World's Best Poets*, World of Poetry; 'If', 2006, *Yellow Moon*; 'The Clash of Life', 1998, *The Liquid Mirror*, International Library of Poetry; 'Still a Good Idea', 2006, *Positive Words*; 'A Little Will Do You Good', 2011, *The Write Angle*; 'When', 2010, *The Mozzie*; 'Different, Yet The Same', 'Stirring the Embers', 'The Cedars in July', 'Poetry At The Cedars', 2011, *That Which My Eyes See*, Ginninderra Press; 'Port Adelaide,1853 – I'm getting quite accustomed to the sight of everything', 'Treasures Old and New', 'Life, and Death, In the River', 2011, *The Heart of Port Adelaide*, Ginninderra Press; 'Great Tales Are Often Told', 2006, *Yellow Moon*; 'The Kookaburra's Tail', 2006, *Ornanthology*, Adelaide Plains Poets; 'Kookaburra', 2006, *Yellow Moon*; 'Our Old Gum Tree', 2006, *Ornanthology*, Adelaide Plains Poets.

On Thinking About It
ISBN 978 1 74027 774 7
Copyright © text John R. Sabine 2012
The cover photo is of the author's granddaughter, Alice, on Ohope Beach, Bay of Plenty, New Zealand, as taken by her mother, Rebecca Sabine, and used with her permission. The image provided the inspiration for the poem 'Girl at the Beach' (page 52).

First published 2012
Reprinted 2015

GINNINDERRA PRESS
PO Box 3461 Port Adelaide SA 5015
www.ginninderrapress.com.au

Contents

On poetry	7
On explaining poetry (to the very young)	9
On time	11
The Ancient Thread: go tell your tales, old man	13
Time Heals All	15
Time, gentlemen, please	16
As my day lengthens	17
There is a softness in the sky	18
On life	19
The Clash of Life	21
The Awareness of Self: does a bird know it is a bird?	23
Still a Good Idea	24
A little will do you good…but a lot will kill you	26
Have a Great Day	27
When	28
Crafty sick	29
Depression	30
Boonta	31
Don't ruminate, my friend, don't ruminate	32
Whyfor War	33
Ah, Cholesterol	35
On Being Politically Correct	36
A flower upon the wall?	38
On love	39
Loving you	41
The merest thought of you	42
The night, it is made for love	43
There is a softness	44
Birds of My Heart	45
A father's destiny	46

On family and friends	47
The Family Farm at Eltham North	49
The Quality Barber at Tusmore Gate	50
Our Citizen of the Year	51
Girl at the Beach	52
On 'The Cedars'	55
Not a hope	57
Different, yet the same	58
Stirring the embers	59
The Cedars in July	60
Poetry at The Cedars	61
On Port Adelaide	63
Port Adelaide, 1853: I'm getting quite accustomed to the sight of everything	65
Treasures old and new	67
Life, and Death, in the River	69
A confession	70
On the sunny side of life	71
I feel an idea coming on	73
Companions All	74
By Any Other Name	76
Good shot, said the 'keeper	77
Epigrams	78
On the bush	79
The Kookaburra's Tail	81
What Can You See in a Dead Gum Tree?	82
Kookaburra	84
Why the Wombat Has a Hairy Nose	85
The Story of the Yellow-tailed Black Cockatoo	87
The Magpie: a debate	88
Our Old Gum Tree	89

On poetry

On explaining poetry (to the very young)

You are a poet, I know,
but Daddy, what do you do?
Words, my son, just words;
but with all the colours of the rainbow,
they're magic.

You are a poet, you say,
but Daddy, what do you do?
Words, my son, only words;
but with all the music of the earth and sky,
they're magic,

But if you are a poet, as so you tell me,
then Daddy, what actually do you do?
Who knows, my son? I don't.
I conjure with words
and if the stars align,
then a story appears.
It's magic, my son, just magic

On time

The Ancient Thread: go tell your tales, old man

There is a thread, an ancient and venerable thread,
maybe strong, maybe not, maybe old and frayed,
but there is never a doubt that it is always there;
links the old and tried with the young and strong,
links the now of today with the know of yesterday.
We are lost without it, and of its spinning no one can shirk.
So tell your tales, old man, for that is now your final work.

Leave out some reflection, neglect a story or miss a memory
and surely then a vital strand of the ancient thread unwinds,
and that collected narrative, that binding fabric of our society
will be all the thinner, both the warp and the weft be weaker;
a colour will be paler, a pattern forever blurred and indistinct.
That scene will go, a hole forever, unless you heed our ask.
So tell your tales, old man, for that is now your final task.

How can that collective sum of our ancestral memory,
that distinctive social cloth that gives reason to our lives,
how can it hold us, bind us, join us all together, united,
unless it is forever being renewed, reworked, rewound;
unless each and every generation plays in turn its role,
combs and cards, spins and weaves, on that collective tapestry?
So tell your tales, old man, for that is now your final destiny.

Not just, though especially, your own offspring but all of us
need to know our place and role, our key refining definition,
that ancient thread that takes for us the reality that is today
back through the hallowed shades and shapes of time and
   place.
Who else but you now holds that pattern, in mind and heart
   and soul?
So tell your tales, old man, go spread your memories abroad.
That now, old man, is both your obligation and your life's
   reward.

Time Heals All

Time heals all, or so they say,
Time to cleanse the hurt and tears;
But will time forever keep at bay
Those memories that fuel my fears?
Is time enough to smooth the rough
Or will it always call my bluff?

Time heals all, or so they tell.
Yet what is time but rate of change?
Must I change as well to break that spell,
To bring my senses back in range?
Time cures, I know it must be so,
How else could I endure the blow?

Time heals all, or so I've heard,
Time to wipe a slate of mem'ries clean;
For time is the cure by all preferred
To dim those stars my heart has seen.
Of course it's true, I must believe anew,
How else to cure my soul of you?

Time, gentlemen, please

Should ever I think that I'm too old to learn,
or take fresh steps on new and different paths,
or feel too weak to work outside the box or square,
to venture forth without the need of map and compass,
then rightly, my friends, my time indeed has run.

Should ever I swear that I'm too old to dare,
to skip and jump and ride, to have some fun,
or feel too worn to keep at least some pace,
along with the young and the younger still,
then truly, my friends, I've really done my dash.

Should ever I state that I'm too old to date,
to laugh and sing and dance the night away;
or believe too spent to write of a better world,
or pen some new and sharper rhymes and rhythms,
then clearly, my friends, my own last word is writ.

Should ever I deem that I'm too old to dream,
to go see the world in new and different ways;
should I ever decide that I'm too weak to try
out new and different parts upon life's stage,
then sadly, my friends, I surely must be done.

Should ever I say that I'm too old to pray,
to dream and still to know that dreams come true,
or ever consider that I'm too late for love,
too spent to give myself for someone else,
then simply, my friends, my own last time is nigh.

As my day lengthens

As I walk, still walking, along the sands of time
the ocean on my left is rolling, roaring, comforting;
while right and front there's still a vast and undiscovered land,
beckoning, where there is yet so much to see, to do, to be.

Who says my steps are slower now? I just take care
not to pass on by those shapes and sounds and colours
that so easily I may have simply missed before,
in days of a faster pace, at another place gone by.

Should I wonder or worry that my joints are creaking,
my eyes, my ears, my muscles are just that little weaker,
for my mind and my heart are firm, can still be put to use?
Are there some who still have need for what yet I have to give?

So as I walk these sands of time I still have time to pray
that there might yet be light enough for me to see the way,
and strength enough and heart enough for me to serve
in faith and love some at least who walk along behind.

There is a softness in the sky

There is a softness in the sky, that time of day
when breezes stir within the garden treetops;
those birds here now, chattering but winding down,
as my voice too sinks quieter, calmer in its tone.

There is a stillness in the air, that evening time,
day's heat has gone, night's cool is yet to come;
one's work is done, though not quite finished,
for more can be tried, more yet that can be done.

There is a softness to the light, that time of day
when sunset colours start to play across the sky;
bright red will sink to pink and then to purple,
though a glow still stays, still shows what's left to do.

There is a stillness to the light, that evening time,
when someone, somewhere, will soon be calling me;
not to cease what I am doing but still to keep on moving.
At the edge of time much joy remains in living, in loving.

On life

The Clash of Life

I'm easing home across the hills and angling west to a sinking sun,
When suddenly in a clash of wills two hawks are at it, one on one,
With flashing wings and slashing bills – to fight all night, for pride won't run.

They wheel and rise and go much higher, then turn and peel into a dive
That streaks the sun with a flash of fire; they swoop on up that each may strive
To make the cast they each desire – could either one remain alive?

But just as swiftly as the fight began, one was struck with a telling blow
And then as vanquished turned and ran, a desperate glide to the void below
Far from the sun and the eyes of man – to the haven only darkness could bestow.

But the victor rose once more on high, to salute in triumph the fading light,
As though into the sinking sun to fly, to cut its rays with glistening might,
To stake his claim to all the sky – then turned and streaked beyond my sight.

As I turned to follow the homeward trail, the red of the sun was almost done,
But that clash of hawks, one strong, one frail, had asked of me would I be brave or run,
Would I in the clash of life prevail – to make my glory flash in the sinking sun?

The Awareness of Self: does a bird know it is a bird?

(The case of the eagle and the hummingbird)

A bird is a bird is a bird,
a statement that is far from absurd.

The gift of life is to soar on high,
to open one's wings to all the sky;
to climb and to swoop and to fly,
to view the world through an eagle's eye.

The gift of life is to smell the flowers,
perfume sweetened by recent showers;
to attend to them all, yours and ours,
these are a hummingbird's finest powers.

A bird is a bird is a bird,
a statement far from absurd,
for to know thyself when doubt is rife
is to seek for meaning within one's life.

The eagle out from its mountain nest
is beholden to no other's behest;
turns the wind to its own request,
rules the sky from east to west.

The hummingbird knows the scent
of a thousand blossoms, heaven sent;
knows the role for which each is meant,
this is a hummingbird's special bent.

A bird is a bird is a bird,
a statement far from absurd,
for to discover your goal within yourself,
gives much meaning to one's own true self.

Still a Good Idea

Now here's a way to live your day,
to keep your life free of strife,
should ever you care to try.
It won't kill you,
may even thrill you,
if you would but dare to try.

Not so easy, that's a fact,
just to keep your soul intact,
not a duty, only sweet and fruity,
every day to do indeed, one simple deed,
an unpremeditated act
of kindness or of beauty.

Think of the difference you could make,
big or small, give or take,
a simple thing indeed.
Just find, within your heart and mind,
to try each day, some kind
or beauty deed.

A word, a smile,
you needn't go the final mile.
Just think about the pleasure,
a little treasure in the sun,
that you could bring along, right along,
with just a little kindness done.

Or if it's elegance that you admire,
to things of beauty you aspire,
then seek it out with fire.
And in the dross that comes your way
you could discover, then recover,
what is gold, not loss, within your day.

So don't delay as you go your way,
every day, at work or play,
with just a little tact
try an unpremeditated act,
of kindness or of beauty.
For joy, not duty.

A little will do you good…but a lot will kill you

The world, we're told, is full of magic cures,
of lotions and notions, sacred herbs and extracts,
of foods and fads; pills, potions and subtle lures,
to cure all ills, from pigeon toes to cataracts.

So you ask your doctor is it good for you;
will it solve your problems, cure your ills
will it ease your bunions and fix the flu,
or will it make you worse, with all those bills.

Whatever the complaint you tackle, you can be sure,
whether to remove some fat, or ease the ageing curse,
whenever you look so hard for that miracle cure
just note, a little is good – but too much is worse.

For that is the trouble, no matter the question,
no matter the food, nor no matter the fad;
the answer is always yes, without exception;
for truly a little is good – but then more is bad.

You want an answer that's sharp and shorter,
try yes; or no; for it is the exact same plot;
whether whisky or wine, or arsenic or water,
whatever, a little is good – but a lot is not.

Have a Great Day

To leap and jump and chase and run,
Up and down and round for fun;
Or just to sit and snooze, relax and drink,
Pretending all the while to think,
So many things that can be done,
In the sun.

One can sit and watch it run the windowpane,
Or listen to it gurgle down the drain.
But one should never sit and fret,
Just step outside and get resounding wet.
For that's the way to clear the brain,
In the rain.

Though clouds may threaten and winds may blow,
With thunder and lightning too for all you know,
'Tis never the time for staying inside,
Nor worrying about a place to hide,
For this is the time to get up and go,
In the snow.

You may consider that you have sinned,
Because you feel the devil has grinned,
But that should not at all delay,
Your entry out in to the fray
All your doubts you can rescind
In the wind

When

When morning comes and brings no sense of hope,
and life feels cold and wan, you lack desire;
when struggling on it's just too hard to cope
and oft the day begins bereft of fire;
when wells clog up, when all your streams have dried
and all your avenues are closed or blocked;
when needing light to shine upon your woes
and every door seems shut and tightly locked;
when all your options come up hard and rough
and every plan is foiled and all hope fails;
when being close is never near enough
and darkest evening comes as sunset pales;
when all around there seems are prison bars
then know, you need the dark to see the stars.

Crafty sick

Shakespeare said it first, Henry IV, Part 2,
when Rumour openly declared anew,
that Northumberland wasn't ill at all; the sly old prick
was simply having us on; he was just being crafty sick.

So now when you call to work and ask for leave,
the boss is not to know what tricks are up your sleeve.
You tell him how your health is less than quite fantastic,
but I know you know the ropes, you're just being crafty sick.

You see it too in Canberra each and every day,
where all of the nation's pollies swap and sway,
and try to bluff the public with some fancy politic.
But they're not fooling me, they're just being craft sick.

Or even when your iPod, your PC or your television
seems down and out, or maybe needs revision,
you think they're broke, or crashed, it's all a trick:
just like you and me, they're just being crafty sick.

Depression

Depression
is no transgression,
is not an obsession
nor suppression of aggression.
So look up, my friend,
don't close up nor cover up
just lift up and lighten up,
loosen up and liven up.
For by confession and digression
you'll beat regression and recession,
you'll make your own progression;
to clear up depression!

Boonta

The natives here know well the signs of it,
the natives here have a fancy name for it,
when your brain cells quit and disappoint ya.
Lose your marbles, then you've gone boonta.

You see those hoons out roaming on the street,
there is not a one that you'd want to meet;
don't let them anywhere near your daughter,
you can plainly see, they've all gone boonta.

The telly has those damned reality shows,
each and every one gets up your nose;
for no matter who might be the presenter
they're all the same, they've all gone boonta.

Our politicians are raving and screaming,
without a clue in their wildest dreaming;
they are forever blabbering under water,
you can easily tell, they've all gone boonta.

I hear my children's voices night and day,
and what is it that I hear my children say?
Doctors ought to lock him up, they really oughta.
Our old man's gone, he's gone completely boonta.

Don't ruminate, my friend, don't ruminate

Psychiatrists do warn us
rumination could harm us;
thus –

If it seems to you that all your life's on hold,
There's nothing left that's big nor brave nor bold,
Don't forsake the action, don't go into traction,
Just wait while I elaborate, let me here enumerate,
But whatever you do don't ruminate, my friend, don't ruminate.

If it seems you've hit the slough of your despond,
And the day is just too dark for anyone to respond,
Then crank up all your gears, lay aside your fears,
Learn to calculate or concentrate, gyrate or germinate,
But whatever you do don't ruminate, my friend, don't ruminate.

If the sun's gone down and the moon's not out,
If all that is left seems hardly worth the shout.
Then pick up all your tools, bone up on the rules,
Adjudicate or arbitrate, dominate or decimate,
But whatever you do don't ruminate, my friend, don't ruminate.

If it seems your life at last is drawing to a close,
If through your soul you sense a chill wind blows,
Then call up the relatives, dream up alternatives,
Neither hesitate nor vacillate, throw away barbiturate,
But whatever you do don't ruminate, my friend, don't ruminate.

Whyfor War

Wherefore war, whyfor war,
it seems it must be happening
somehow, somewhere, sometime, all the time.
It seems there is an urge that's violent,
unexplained and inexplicable,
that drives, predominantly the male, in his prime.
Why go, why not,
what else is there to do,
when strikes that madness of mind and whim?
Someone calls, yells, screams,
some crap-happy politician demands,
allegiance, completely, from everyone but him.
You want Afghanistan, go take it.
You crave the oil that's in Iraq,
there's only a piddling war to stop your run.
You want the Palestinian mess,
the Irish, though, have paused for breath,
bugger, someone else is having all the fun.
Wherever you like in Africa,
north or south or in the middle,
guns and kids today are surely blazing.
Biafra, Darfur, up and down
the Nile, the Congo or Zambezi,
charge on you bastards, fight, all hell is raising.
So still you crave the deadly action,
you cannot live without your cordite fix;
stupid prick, those wars belong on someone else's card.
Go armed here locally instead, be a man instead,
even half a man would do, if you but could
stomach the fight right here, in our own backyard.
Somewhere someone may be winning,

but sure as hell we're losing here,
because we've mostly chickened out; who gives a shit.
From the war on poverty, and drugs,
on disease, the environment, on ignorance and crime,
from the fight for Aboriginal rights, oh brother, we've mostly quit.
Now don't blame Little Johnny, or Kevin 07,
demand another style of leader, you,
for these are the battles we need to fight and not retreat,
these are the wars that we need to win,
right here, not in some goddamn hellhole overseas.
Fight on the home front, man. Else we all go down, and in defeat.

Ah, Cholesterol

Ah cholesterol, why all this fuss,
what in fact have you done to us?
Why sure, you clog our veins and arteries,
you raise our blood pressure and lower our hopes;
but then again you also keep intact
all of our cellular membranes
and keep all of our nerves in tune;
our brains as well, they really do have need of you;
and you are too the starting stuff for us to make
some of our liver juices, all of our sexy hormones.
So why then, cholesterol, how come all the fuss,
with all that good work, indeed, that you do for us?

On Being Politically Correct

You mustn't smoke, you mustn't eat fat,
when out in the sun you must wear a hat;
you must go steady when on the grog,
be ready to clean up after your dog;
for surely my friend, you really must see,
politically correct is the only way to be –
oh yes, politically correct is the only way to be.

When hiring someone, watch for the hex.
that someone must be of the opposite sex,
or you'll be caught for discrimination,
there'll be some sad recrimination;
for surely my friend, you really must know
politically correct is the only route to go –
oh yes, politically correct is the only route to go.

Should you ever engage those awful bores
who forever are fighting the history wars,
cross swords with a literary deconstructionist
or try talking sense with a rabid creationist,
then surely my friend, no need to be told
politically correct is the only view to hold –
oh yes, politically correct is the only view to hold.

When discussing whatever remotely religious,
expressing an opinion on people indigenous,
take note and be careful, especially be sure
that whatever you say is ethnically so pure,
for surely my friend, if really you care
politically correct is the only fare, I swear –
oh yes, politically correct is the only fare; beware.

So, where's the buzzness, oh where's the fizzness,
politically correct is so terribly bad for business;
we'll all be poor, that is for sure,
nobody smokes here any more.

A flower upon the wall?

This I'm seeing, is this all,
just a flower, a photo on a wall?
some colours splashed,
a few shapes dashed
into the brightest light;
a clear and simple sight.

Or hidden in this flower
do I sense some power,
a message in its beauty,
perhaps another quality,
a subtle majesty of form,
unique, beyond the norm.

This did the Lord create
and is ours to appreciate,
He put it there in nature
for you and I to nurture,
to lift our minds above
and our hearts to love.

On love

Loving you

Loving you,
Trying to be true,
Loving you,
Just the neatest thing to do.

Love in the morning
Welcomes the dawning.
Love in the morning

Love in the evening
Cancels all grieving,
Love in the evening

Love in the night time,
Always the right time,
Love in the night time.

Loving you,
Trying to be true,
Loving you,
Just the greatest thing to do.

The merest thought of you

The merest thought of you, my love, is quite enough
To send my heart into a spin;
The energy you radiate can cross the world
And turn my night to brightest day.

The slightest sound of you, my love, upon the phone,
And I am all a quiver,
The resonance of your voice, my love, is sweet indeed,
And lovelier than ought that I can say.

The softest taste of you, my love, within my mouth,
Fills me full unto the brim,
The firmness of your breasts, my love, so turns me on,
That in your hands I am the softest clay.

The lightest touch of you, my love, against my flesh,
Goes arrow straight into my heart;
The warmth of your embrace, my love, and I am lost,
Within the wonder of your way.

The sweetest grip you take, my love, upon my shaft,
As I am plunged within your depths,
The chemistry we share, my love, is gold to me
And precious jewels now here to stay.

The night, it is made for love

Through a day of fun in the tropical sun
We played together, stayed together,
Your eyes were glowing, laughter flowing
But the night, it is made for love.

When the sun was high in the tropical sky,
Your hand held mine, that was fine,
Your hair was flashing, your body smashing
But the night, it is made for love.

Then I hold you tight on a tropical night
For I need you near, but closer my dear,
For the sun is sinking and I am thinking
That the night, it is made for love

'Tis never too soon, there's a tropical moon.
Just hold me close, your love is a dose
Of sweetest dreaming, forever meaning
That the night, it is made for love.

There is a softness

There is a softness to the air,
A breeze that gently stirs the night,
That whispers sweetly through your hair,
And catches you against the light.

There is a softness to the sky
For now that light is fading fast,
A star or two appear up high,
And you are in my arms at last.

There is a softness to your touch,
A smile that lingers on your lips,
That lightens up your eyes so much
Adds sweetness to your finger tips.

There is a softness to your love,
So trustingly do we embrace,
That from my position just above
I can see that love upon your face.

Birds of My Heart

I see the lakeside birds in flight,
I see them rise in dawn's soft light.
They climb so swift on dew-heavy air,
Would that my heart could join them there.

For I hear them calling across the gorges
To mates responding in a love that forges.
Where is my mate to share my call along,
A gorge of love to echo back my song?

The light's now bright and the birds have flown,
But my heart stays stuck on the ground alone,
For there is no strength that I can find
To bring relief to my heart or mind.

And yet, and yet, the sun is in the air,
It flicks with flame the hilltops bare,
With light and warmth along the lake
To grow and glow…for my heart's sake?

And thus if my soul could only know
That come one dawn a light would grow,
Some other song for my heart to run
Some other love to catch the sun;
Are you…that one?

A father's destiny

When a babe arrives, then so too does fatherhood arrive;
so now, as baby strives to grow and learn and do, then just so too
must a father learn to do, what may – or may not – come naturally.
To provide for the body is a simple task, just money to be earned,
and saved, a shelter made, a home and a hearth to be sustained;
but for the needs of the heart and the mind and the soul
of his newborn, a father must find a whole new range of skills, of talents,
for a whole new person must this freshly-minted father now maintain.

For now there is willow to be bent and cured,
steel to be forged, and shaped, and welded;
there is a new heart to be loved, to be filled with love,
a mind to be introduced to the wonders of earth and sky,
a soul to be crafted to know of right and wrong and responsibility,
a character to be nurtured and cherished, with its own new life;
all that, when babe arrives, so too arrives a father's destiny.

On family and friends

The Family Farm at Eltham North

There once was land, farming land,
then not quite a century old;
orchards there and all around,
early fruit for the Melbourne market.

There once was land, orchard land,
of apples and peaches, apricots too;
the yellow you see were quinces,
early to blossom in the Eltham spring.

There once was land, dairying land,
trees giving place to milking cows;
in early memories, those placid beasts,
were all ruled over by a Jersey bull.

There once was land, grazing land,
cows and bull replaced by steers;
horses too, brought there to graze,
as land and Cousin Jim both got older.

There once was land, family land,
in Murray hands for a hundred years
and more, till development now prevailed
and houses sit, where once was farming land.

The Quality Barber at Tusmore Gate

Any topic you care to name, just to fit today's time frame,
simple or complex are all fair game, to us it's all the same,
we cover all with dash and dare, with words we're debonair,
with my just sitting there, as David the barber cuts my hair.

Religion or politics are simply fine, nowhere do we draw the line,
however the world is in decline, its troubles or just his and mine;
our scope is truly everywhere, every topic both fit and fair,
never a reason for despair, if David the barber cuts my hair.

No fancy salon de coiffure this stop, just a humble barber's shop,
with just my hair to comb and lop, simple styling sides and top,
and the joy of sitting there, strangers never stop and stare,
who cares what I wear, while David the barber cuts my hair.

Time itself might have to wait, time for us to contemplate
the lines of our respective fate, time for us to ruminate;
all that time with nary a care, sitting in a favourite chair,
to emerge with extra flair, when David the barber cuts my hair.

Our Citizen of the Year

She treads so softly on the grass, always by a smile preceded,
Never lets an occasion pass, helps wherever help is needed;
Volunteers when e'er she can, she always goes that extra mile,
Always follows through her plan and does it all with style.
A person whom we all hold dear, one from whom all Burnside learns,
For now she is our Citizen of the Year, she is our Shirley Burns.

Take care, she says, take care, for that is what the world requires,
Join me, she says, and dare to care for what you see transpires
In the wide environment outside, or just within your neighbourhood,
For problems are there and they don't hide, they must be understood.
Yes she is the one we all should hear, we too should take our turns,
For now she is our Citizen of the Year, she is our Shirley Burns.

Now she's on the campaign trail, if biodiversity or cleaner streams we need,
Or caring for the elderly and frail, she thinks outside the square indeed,
While pushing the envelope to its limits, she volunteers but never nags,
Who else has all these merits, and also rids the world of plastic bags?
About her we can indeed be clear, our accolades she clearly earns,
For she is now our Citizen of the Year, she is our Shirley Burns.

Girl at the Beach

Where are you standing, little girl,
out there in sunshine and sea,
you are a long way off, perhaps,
yet still close by to me;
to all the world it would but seem
that you are on your own,
and yet I'm sure that you can feel
and know you're not alone;
our love is flowing for you to sense
and there for you to know,
as you feel the morning's breeze
and glimpse the water's glow.

What are you thinking, little girl,
more than a simple day of fun,
as you gaze upon those doubled clouds,
and look into the rising sun;
can you tell for us, little one, is the tide
going out or coming back in,
or can you not yet feel that ebb and flow,
that pull upon your skin;
is it meeting you or leaving you
to greet the distant sky;
what more of life is here for you to learn
today…and more to wonder why.

Where are you going, little girl,
in rippling wave and water,
at some part of the start of a journey,
my small and lovely daughter;
what I can see through the camera lens,
is a seascape wide and sweeping
or do you take in some other scene, a challenge,
though well within your keeping;
why in this expanding dawn do you seem
to pause and contemplate,
with light in front and love behind, little girl,
you have no need to hesitate.

On 'The Cedars'

Not a hope

When today I stand in awe
of genius that shows no flaw
and claim to be a poet,
'tis silly, I know it,
no words of mine could ever match that which Sir Hans did
   paint or draw.

Different, yet the same

Is it much the same for you as for me? What do I imagine
when I close my eyes and think, ah yes, Heysen;
mostly, though of course rather vague and indistinct,
farms in the Adelaide hills, eucalypts in late afternoon,
man and beast, say, on *The Way Home, Billy Goat Lane*,
wearily both, for the day had been hot and the work hard;
the colours too, muted, dusty, indistinct perhaps, greens
and browns, flecks of white, bleached by the Australian sun.

But I am wrong, of course. That same Heysen eye and hand,
that same Heysen skill with line and length and light,
did just as readily and just as remarkably capture
very different scenes in very different times and places;
though the *Dutch luggers on the coast of Scotland*,
are bleached more by ocean storms than midday sun;
it is all there, a familiar figure, a sense of distance; a different
scene, different setting, but pleasure for me the same. And for
   you?

Stirring the embers

Sketches, in charcoal and chalk and conte orange,
more resonant to me when expressed on toned paper,
images of times and of lives long since passed,
of sheds and a barn, of cattle and sheep and horses,
of *Turning the Plough* and *Mending the Harrow*,
these stir alight the still-warm embers of my memory.

Here displayed in a studio, where stone and wood abound,
a more substantial version, perhaps, of *Thiele's Barn*;
more solid indeed than *The Artist's First Studio*,
it too reminds me of earlier days that I have known;
building and drawings, in this particular setting,
all stir a glow in the still-warm embers of my memory.

For I knew and lived and loved in such structures,
worked with horses and wagons and cattle like these,
when I was but a boy, visiting our cousin's farm;
this landscape too, the hills of Adelaide's Hahndorf,
reflecting the hills of my own Melbourne's Eltham,
all now stirring fire in the still-warm embers of my memory.

The Cedars in July

Mystical;
today, a winter scene in the cold and the wind and the rain,
today, viewed through the homestead window pane,
these paddocks are those the artist saw, these great trees the same,
but today they take on a softer hue, are set within a differing frame,
than many his summer landscapes show; with this pale light at play,
not so much *Red Gold*, as *Frosty morning, Edwards farm* I see today;
magical.

Poetry at The Cedars

I see them now upon these homely walls,
framed images, just as Heysen captured them,
of these same hills, these trees, these tracks,
these animals and people and places,
mostly golden in the glory of a dying sun;
telling stories not just of one day done,
but of many days, many ways, long gone.

As I stand in awe of one man's skill,
images from the past, yet still ever present,
I look to see if I too could glimpse that vision;
if I perhaps could capture in some simple words,
some faint echo of those scenes, in poetry, today,
that he expressed so eloquently, in earlier days,
in paint and watercolour, in chalk and charcoal.

But was it not indeed a poet who said,
he doubted that he would ever see,
a poem near as lovely as a tree?
and he had not seen these trees that I now see,
through the eyes of the master painter.
Eucalypts mostly, few elm or oak or even cedar,
all glowing, mostly, in the rays of the evening sun;
so now I know no poem of mine, dear reader,
could match in loveliness the art that he has done.

On Port Adelaide

Port Adelaide, 1853: I'm getting quite accustomed to the sight of everything

We arrived at the Port
& moored at 7 o'clock,
several ships were in harbour
& one steamer.

The fourteenth of March 1853,
one hundred twenty-six days out
from Gravesend, England,
great-grandfather Clement found
Port Adelaide, distant
eight miles from the city,
is as might be expected
a dirty and dusty place;
the people living there
are of the lowest class,
generally hawkers and sailors;
the Post Customs House
a poor kind of place.

Though not all at the Port
was without appeal,
bought some grapes 4d per lb,
which greatly refreshed us;
nor all of the architecture
to be condemned,
facing the principal moorings a row
of very good & commodious warehouses.
Yet still he worried,
behind these streets is the Episcopalian
place of worship, a poor edifice;
an Independent Chapel is near to it,
likewise a meagre building.

But while March that year was harsh and dry,
by the last of May he would tell us now
quite a different tale.

*I can already see that I have been incorrect
in many things I have here written
about the Port, Adelaide, & the Country
but I suppose it was very well
compiled after only a transitory
passage thro' these places.*

For by then
*Winter has almost set in;
the grass is growing,
and I am getting quite accustomed
to the sight of everything.*

Lines in italics are direct quotations from Clement Sabine's diary,
held in the South Australian State Library

Treasures old and new

It is surely a sad but familiar tale the whole world over,
just how do we build the new and yet not lose the old;
how do we freshen our lands in the framework of today
without destroying the undoubted charms of yesterday?

Must the Adelaide Milling Company Limited just quietly
disappear,
must we lose forever that grand old flour mill, all five stories
high,
must the lifeblood of the old and working port of a century
past
make way for luxury living in the new Port, think Newport
Quays?

There, as elsewhere in the Port, disused railway lines still
gleam,
Through grass and weeds and poor-laid bitumen;
To remind us still of the glory of a working port,
Surely there still is room for this, need for this today?

The Wharf Hotel was once right there, at number 15 Todd
Street,
in my ancestor's time, newly-built and by then quite
flourishing;
some twenty pubs in the 1850s, seventy-five or more by
century's end;
The Wharf and all but a dozen now sadly gone, and mostly
forgotten.

Yes we do still have, and rightly so, a brace of memorials built,
special structures to honour those sons and daughters from
   the Port,
lost while fishing at sea, appropriately, or fighting in foreign
   wars;
but buildings we built should also stay, for they hold memories
   too.

There once was a wise and humble man, who said that the
   kingdom of heaven
was like unto a vast storehouse that held many treasures,
   both old and new;
our challenge for the Port today is to hold in this same regal
   harmony
both the treasures of old we inherit and the treasures we
   newly create.

Life, and Death, in the River

The Port Adelaide River, for so long,
the working heart and soul of the Port,
attracted all of the early commerce,
attracting still so many visitors today.
A stubby lighthouse upon the dock
drew those early sailors in,
while the play of tumbling porpoises
creates the draw card of today.

But that same great river and harbour,
working so well for the life of the state,
can also harbour future danger
in the form of one unwanted visitor.
Seagrass meadows on its bed, and
their breeding stocks of feeder fish,
even porpoises too may disappear
if we are anything less than careful.

All are threatened by a noxious plant,
A very invasive saltwater seaweed.
Caulerpa toxifolia, arrived ten years ago
and threatens now a whole fish industry;
and so the fight for the Port's survival goes on
but now in the water too, as well as on the shore.
Watch our boats and gear, don't spread it,
if we see it, report it; eternal vigilance
is truly the price of our liberty here,
a charge that surely all of us owe
to a beloved Port Adelaide and river.
As to its people too, both old and new.

A confession

It was only a simple escapade,
but will I need some legal aid?
For surely such a terrible crime,
Will doubtless have me doing time,
to have written such awful rhyme about beloved Port Adelaide.

On the sunny side of life

I feel an idea coming on

Slowly it rises
from out of the pile, other stuff
all previously dumped and rolled and covered, the lot
protected from birds and beasts and you and me.
Like an old, discarded and long-buried tyre,
slowly, but slowly easing its way to the surface;
each pass of the 'dozer inching it up
until – pop – there it is once more,
on top of the pile. But still of no real worth;
no longer do they bury them under the earth.

Just so, occasionally,
does some old and long-buried idea float slowly up
from the murky depths of my memory dump;
the passing pressure, just time this time,
easing down on surrounding, long-discarded stuff
so that this once-forgotten gem (oh yes)
now sits, renewed, upon the surface
and far removed from the uselessness
it might have been then.
Please, don't bury it again.

Companions All

If ever you feel you have run the course,
Have filled your time without remorse,
Don't ever believe the end's in view
And there's nothing more for you to do,
Till you have felt the warming force,
Of a horse!

If you think you're just the smallest cog
In life's machinery, or just one lonely log
That's floating along in an awful jam,
If life is just one battering ram,
Even if it's nought but fog.
Get a dog!

If you can be the sort that truly loves a hat,
Though it may be old and battered and flat,
Then if you are looking in your old age
For comfort and ease upon life's stage,
You can have much more than that.
Love a cat!

If your aims in life seem all deferred
And you're just moving with the herd;
If life can seem to pass you by
When you really want to fly,
Then don't you be deterred.
Find a bird!

If you feel there's nothing more to relish,
Neither fun nor fill in cup nor dish,
And yet you want to conquer strife
And you want much more from life.
Then this will fill your every wish.
Rent a fish.

If you find your ship is left behind in dock
You're just a chip from someone else's block,
Now don't you worry that you need depend
Upon any furred or feathered friend,
For truly you can put your stock,
In a rock!

By Any Other Name

When you recall how all your senses froze,
When first you plucked and put it to your nose,
Where in all the world could one presume
To find the fount of such perfume,
Could it be ought else, do you suppose,
Than a rose.

When first you see a spark that glows
A flash of fire and fun that flows,
Within your heart and within hers too,
A bond that means so much to you,
Infuse a joy from top to toes,
Give a rose.

When you know you have a love that grows
A love that ne'er a boundary knows,
Yet there is still a need to find
A way to say what's on your mind
Then give what every love bestows,
It's a rose.

When from some friend all spirit goes,
And if from him all life force flows,
You have a need that's quite profound
Yet words you want can scarce be found
There's all the grief you can compose,
In a rose.

Good shot, said the 'keeper

Good shot, said the 'keeper.
Good shot! good grief,
how different from the sledging of now;
but then, in my day, that was cricket.
And indeed it was a good shot,
as in my mind, after fifty years,
I can still play that one again;
a fast ball rising, outside the line,
on my toes with a perfect cut; four;
just that once, bat meeting ball full on
and singing in the sweetest harmony;
just that once, on one of those rare days;
for I was no batsman, oh no,
no centuries for me, a twenty perhaps,
and I would be over the moon.
And that day, yes, good shot said the 'keeper.
Yet as I re-live that memory over and over
its sweetness is tinged with remembered dismay;
for in my exhilaration, good shot said the 'keeper,
but thank you, in turn, I had neglected to say.

Epigrams

Modern poetry

Now new-style poetry is all in season,
though it has not rhyme nor rhythm nor reason.
Yet to inform the chattering critics upon their knees
that in such new clothes the emperor poet will freeze
is still just regarded as so much treason.

Great tales of old

Great tales are often told
of the glorious knights of old,
of wars that were lost and kingdoms won,
of marvellous deeds triumphant done.
But what of daytime fun?

When all is said and done

Since when all is said and done,
more is usually said than done,
no wonder that instruction books
never shows the final looks
of a sponge cake overdone.

On the bush

The Kookaburra's Tail

Do you ever listen to the kookaburra's song,
And wonder why it lasts so long?
Then let me tell you all of a wondrous tale,
For there is magic stored in the kookaburra's tail.

Every feather in the tail is a story heard,
All passed around from bird to bird,
From hills and valleys, from coast and dale
They're all to be found in the kookaburra's tail.

With each new song that the kookaburra sings
It tells its mates about all those things,
It laughs at the words and grins at the tale
Every colour is there in the kookaburra's tail.

The blues and the brown, the white and the black,
Across its breast and right down its back,
Every feather that's there has its own special tale,
But the very best shine in the old bird's tail.

For there are stories there of the swagmen of old,
Of squatters and troopers and a bushranger bold,
Of the old and the young, of the strong and the frail,
Every story in the rainbow's found in the kookaburra's tail.

There's one of the city cove stuck forever in the loo,
Of children and horses, of the cow and the kangaroo,
If you wish them spread don't bother with the mail,
For the yarns will go round with the kookaburra's tail.

But when a feather falls out, oh dearie me,
For that is surely a story gone, like a fallen tree.
But no, for another will grow though at first all pale,
Till one more story brings its own special glory
To add to the colours in the kookaburra's tail.

What Can You See in a Dead Gum Tree?

Have ever you noticed along our creeks and rivers, especially,
but up the banks and into the bush beyond, as far as the eye
 can see,
there is bound to be found there many a dead gum tree.
Not just red gums, Manna gums and scrubby gums,
but blue gums, spotted gums and sugar gums too,
snow gums, ghost gums and even a lemon-scented gum or
 two.

Ironbarks, stringy-barks and paperbarks are there,
and boxes too, of every shape and hue,
grey box, red box and yellow box, to name just a few;
wherever kurrajong and coolabah and karri and jarrah
originally did their dash,
from every kind of mallee to the majestic mountain ash.

Just listen with care to the wind in them all, short or tall,
and soon you too will come under their spell,
for they each and all have a wondrous tale to tell.
In the early morn or late afternoon, but best of all with a
 crescent moon,
if your heart is pure you will be sure to hear, today, tomorrow,
the glories of the stories that each one knows,
of life and love, of joy and sorrow,
of the ups and downs in the life of every thing that grows.

And watch them too as the birds come nesting, especially so
the coloured galah and the black and the white cockatoo.
They're not just resting, I promise you that,
as from the wind in the branches they will capture a song
to carry along to the next tree in their track,
and bring one back, the very next day,
or whenever they happen again to be out that way.

And insects too, there are always more than a few,
bush flies and butterflies, bugs and beetles
and many a busy bee, oh can't you see,
they're in every tree but specially the old,
watching and waiting to make the music
for every tale that is told.

So take no chances, just study the branches,
and watch every bird and bee that you can see.
Then when the wind comes blowing
and the clouds are flowing across the sky,
just creep up near and you will hear
your own special legend of the by and by.
For there's much to hear and there's much to see,
in the shapes and the sounds of a dead gum tree.

Kookaburra

Kookaburra
Striking, brown
Calling, singing, laughing
The king of kingfishers
Jackass?

Why the Wombat Has a Hairy Nose

Deep in a hollow, where no one could follow,
lived old-man wombat, just he and his hat;
winter was coming, the bees stopped humming,
his toes were too cold, he was ever so old.

With frost on the ground, and hardly a sound,
there was no one out, not a soul about,
not even his cousin, the last of a dozen,
and the last of the line, a race in decline.

But little he knew, this last of the few,
that within his hat special magic sat.
With weathered old brim, neither neat nor trim
at the sound of a bell it could weave any spell.

Though not any old bell could summon this spell,
just one held in store, never rung before;
that had never been heard, neither beast nor bird,
no creature at all, had perceived its call.

The cold was intense and it made no sense
to be up and about, or let alone out;
yet all of a rush, a strange little thrush,
fell in through his door and rolled on his floor.

Both gave a yell, and it triggered the spell;
a chorus of wombat and bird had never been heard,
their voices together, combined with the weather,
you could easily tell, did sound like a bell.

Wombat's hat seemed to grow, the brim was aglow,
and at once he knew it would surely come true,
any wish he could make for the whole tribe's sake
would surely be granted, its truth implanted.

He wanted the best for himself and the rest
of his family line; with their race in decline,
if he should retire, they would all expire;
'tis an old refrain, not a one would remain.

So he asked for life and a lovely wife
and lots more wombats, but forget their hats.
And so was attested, their decline arrested,
you now see the score, there are wombats galore.

But it came at a price, one not quite nice.
Each wombat knows, their good fortune shows,
for that wintry old spell of the hat and the bell
forever just froze the hairs on their nose.

The Story of the Yellow-tailed Black Cockatoo

Pride, I have heard it said, comes often before a fall,
And those who want too much might lose it all;
And so it was once, when all cockatoos were white
Each spotlessly clean, each bird a glorious sight.

Kings and queens of the sky, all catching the sun,
reflecting its glory as if by their own right won.
yet even then in the midst of all that purity
lingered one who desired some greater surety.

One for whom more than enough was not enough
despite such beauty and grace he craved to be tough;
who needed some sign of being blessed by fate
to be acclaimed by all for his privileged state.

So not content just reflecting those rays of light,
he longed to carry their very source in flight
to have for himself and his clan a piece of the flame,
to proclaim to the world for ever and ever his fame.

The foolish bird in his pride flew close
to the source of the blazing sun's heat
which singed and blackened his feathers,
burned through too the skin of his feet.

So forever a splash of sun colour on their tail
may seem to them like a mark of distinction,
but it also serves to remind them, alas,
that they are close to the brink of extinction.

The Magpie: a debate

So pretty a bird, all blacks and whites,
darting through noon, catching the lights;
weaving through branches, high and low,
with shining eye and feathers aglow;
so pretty the magpie, lovely bird.

Well, bugger the magpie, diving at me,
unexpected, out of a tree.
First felt not seen, so sharp a beak
cracked on my scalp, blood could leak.
So bugger the magpie, vicious bird.

So which is which, friend or foe,
out in the bush, who's to know?
At times so sweet, at others a pest.
Can we just say, the Lord knows best;
so clever the magpie, two-faced bird.

Our Old Gum Tree

The kookaburra laughs a merry old song,
He laughs out loud and he laughs out long,
He lifts his head and he calls with glee
And he makes his home in our old gum tree.

The rosella for true is our prettiest bird,
Though not the sweetest you might have heard,
But his colours are bright as you can see
For he makes his home in our old gum tree.

The dark old crow has a callow old call
That goes way out as warning to all,
So we can tell and leave him free
To make his home in our old gum tree.

Now the bird of state is the piping shrike
What the magpie calls a small lookalike.
But either way you can surely see
They make their home in our old gum tree.

There are cockatoos too and galahs galore,
Wrens and robins and a dozen more;
All swift and sure like the big honeybee
To make their home in our old gum tree.